I0166520

Taking Shape

Taking Shape

carmina figurata

BY

Jan D. Hodge

ABLE MUSE PRESS

Copyright ©2015 by Jan D. Hodge
First published in 2015 by

Able Muse Press

www.ablemusepress.com

All rights reserved. No part of this book may be used or reproduced in any manner whatsoever without written permission except in the case of brief quotations embedded in critical articles and reviews. Requests for permission should be addressed to the Able Muse Press editor at editor@ablemuse.com

Printed in the United States of America

Library of Congress Control Number: 2015937385

ISBN 978-1-927409-56-5 (paperback)
ISBN 978-1-927409-58-9 (hardcover)
ISBN 978-1-927409-57-2 (digital)

Cover image: "Egg Typed" by Alexander Pepple

Cover & book design by Alexander Pepple

Able Muse Press is an imprint of *Able Muse:* A Review of Poetry, Prose & Art—at www.ablemuse.com

Able Muse Press
467 Saratoga Avenue #602
San Jose, CA 95129

Acknowledgments

"A Posy," "Lament for the Maker," "Madonna and Child"
and "Toltec" first appeared in *Able Muse,*
"In Memory: John Bennett" in
The Beloit Poetry Journal, "Salamander" and "Laureate"
in *Buckle &,* "Hélène de Nervo de Montgerould"
in *North American Review,* "Genesis" and
"The One That Got Away" in *New Orleans Review,*
"Wheatstraw" in *Black Bear Review,* "Winner"
in *Susquehanna Quarterly,* "Icon" in *New Trad Journal,*
"Sabbat" and "Veteran's Day" in *Frostwriting,*
and "The Lesson of the Snow" in *Off the Coast.*

"Carousel" won the 1997 WordArt Esme Bradberry Prize
and appears in *Western Wind* (5th ed.), eds. David Mason and
John Frederick Nims (McGraw-Hill, 2006).
Nine of these poems, several in different versions,
appeared in *Poems to be Traded for Baklava*
(the Onionhead Annual chapbook for 1997).

"Pandanggo sa Ilaw" appeared in the essay "Taking Shape:
the Art of *Carmina Figurata,*" in *An Exaltation of Forms,*
eds. Annie Finch and Kathrine Varnes (U. of Michigan Press, 2000).

Preface

My serious interest in the *carmen figuratum,* or shaped poem, was kindled when I read Paul Fussell's comments on George Herbert's "Easter Wings" in his *Poetic Meter and Poetic Form* (rev. ed., New York, Random House, 1979):

> Like most shaped poems it incurs one important artistic disadvantage: it makes an unbalanced sensual appeal—its structure directs itself more to the eye than to the ear. . . . The visual experience of the stanzas has triumphed inharmoniously over their auditory appeal . . . the two dimensions are not married: one is simply in command of the other. . . . The art of *carmen figuratum* is the province perhaps more of the typographer . . . than of the poet. It is in . . . the perfect harmony of . . . visual and auditory logic at the same time that any poem achieves its triumphs.

One might of course argue that poetry is primarily an auditory experience, to which, in this art, a visual dimension is added. But that aside, Fussell also argues:

> Perhaps the greatest limitation of shaped poems . . . is the scarcity of visual objects which they can imitate: . . . wings, bottles, hourglasses, and altars, but where do we go from there?

Looking up from the text, I spotted a spiral candlestick and decided to write a poem in its shape to use as a Christmas card. In that poem,

```
                    A
                   new
                  light
                 is born
                  unto
                   us
                Christmas
                was first
                the Child.
                How  mild
                that face
                of grace.
      From the manger where He lay that night
          poured a radiance which rid
              the world of shade,
              good so profound
              dark was drowned
                 in light!
          Bright angels sang His name
       and a new star blazed above
     and kings and shepherds came
       to that fountainhead of love.
          How gently He rested  there
            in Mary's fair arms gathered
              in that homely stable where
              the ox and ass were tethered.
          They saw such glory flowing
        as bathed the world in balm;
      they had  no way  of  knowing
       what  lay  in store  for  Him,
          for nothing there betokened
            the nails tearing His flesh,
              those precious limbs broken,
            and He hanging on the Cross,
                  and night
       falling in daylight, for His death
        robbed  the very  light  of  breath.
     But He became a child, and died, by right
     that we might share in everlasting light.
```

highly conventional in both subject and style (rhymed, iambic, with deliberately broken rhythm and rhyme at the point of the Crucifixion), I was less strict with spacing than I would be in later poems.

A few years later, listening to a student's piano recital, I was struck by the idea of writing a shaped poem about it. The search for other interesting, usable shapes led to two more poems in the fall of 1991—the sea horse and Columbus's ships, the design for the latter coming from a newspaper advertisement. By then I was hooked, and committed myself to writing a series of *carmina figurata*.

I was familiar with a handful of shaped poems by others (Herbert's "Easter Wings" and "The Altar," several each by May Swenson and John Hollander, and a few others), but discovered Dick Higgins's *Pattern Poetry: Guide to an Unknown Literature* (SUNY Press, 1987), which illustrates many varieties of pattern poetry, only after many of the poems in this collection were written. I had, however, already decided on the "rules" I would follow. I wanted shapes that were intrinsically interesting and particularly appropriate to their subjects, but also wanted the poems to work well *as poems*, using the language itself to create the shapes without varying spacing, compromising syntax for the sake of design, or resorting to typographical tricks. I also chose to write metrically; most of the figures are iambic, though Columbus's ships and the Filipina dancer are anapestic, the salamander is a trochaic chant, and the first carousel horse is dactylic/anapestic.

Obviously line length and line breaks are determined by the shapes rather than more conventional prosodic concerns, but, keeping in mind Fussell's observation about the difficulty of marrying the visual and auditory appeals, I have made few other concessions to the demands of shape. At the same time, those demands led to many possibilities and discoveries, and the interplay between form and idea was a constant source of both frustration and creative tension. I have chosen not to capitalize sentences or to punctuate (except for question marks and in a few other instances), trusting the words and the logic of language to speak for themselves. I have, however, provided brief notes on many of the poems.

My thanks to my father, who long ago taught me his interest in typography, and to those several reader-critics who have over the years encouraged my effort.

J. D. H.

Sioux City, Iowa
December 2014

Contents

Taking Shape

Genesis

for Penny

Pondering Keats's idea that "the imagination may be compared to Adam's dream—he awoke and found it truth," I imagined three versions of the origin of the sea horse, including a new "Greek" myth. With sea horses, the male bears the young.

```
             what        rare
          imagination shaped
       so intricate fantastic delicate
       a creature? from what dream emerged
       to startle sleep this miniature joy
       that floats his prances in a realm
   strange   except in dream? did some benign
  immortal  maker exercise her wit to prompt
 humility  toward bearing young or teach the
scoffers  how delightful grace can be?  or
contrarily  is there a darker    story some
presumption  that a jealous god    resented?
perchance  a sailfish sought to      match
 majesty  with the golden steeds       who
  chariot  the sun across the sky      and
   leaping  tried to catch the sun
    annoyed  by such an act the god
     decreed  that fish that seek to
        rival  steeds would live mere
              parodies of what they
              were or would be pride
              brought low but no we
              want romance imagine
              then one day a dizzy
              colt happy from the
              tang of ferment
              drinking in a
              rill beheld
              a glimpse
              of lively
              fishes in
              a bright       quirky
              quivering     reflection
              and from   that   dream
              was born   the    ideal
              marriage    of   sweet
                 instinct   and a
                  vital innocent
                    surprise
```

Recital

for Michelle McClure

The poem is informed by Copland's piano fantasy "Cat and Mouse." I have tried to capture the spirit of the piece in words, deliberately confusing syntax toward the end to imitate the hectic pace of the music. (Note too that the word "righthand" is the pianist's right hand on the piano.)

```
                         harmonies
                         disarming
                         leisurely
                        are hardly
                       hints of what
                      will softly soon
                     explode  as fingers deftly delicately play at cat
                    and mouse   the quick finesse and dazzling discipline
                   trick chaos  mimic instinct as it trips an ageold dance
                   strike chords   that find their echo deep within us each
       how              we take delight  in what for that poor mouse is terror
      still          why think of him?  all that matters is that he amuse
       the     cat is playing   lefthand tabby  prancing after righthand scampers
      into     meeklysqueaking  hurry-scurries  up down up till lefthand leaps at
    righthand   bright and    spritely teasing  baiting chasing   pause   and in an
   instant  swiftpaw falls   and whispers all  is whiskertwitch and quiver fluff
   and cuff     a fit         of frenzy                              rushing
   hushing as      a          cunning                                paw
   tips out a   C            F                                      A
      a rapid                D                                      G
      one last               B                                      &
        silence              #
```

Pandanggo sa Ilaw

"Pandanggo sa ilaw," the "lamp dance," is a Filipino folk dance in which the dancers balance lighted oil lamps on their hands. *Tutubi* is Tagalog (Filipino) for dragonfly; *makahiya,* the "shy plant," folds up instantly when touched; *sampagita,* the national flower, has small cream blossoms and is often woven into garlands; *magandang babae* means beautiful woman.

Rampa is an irrigation ditch; *balut* (hard-boiled duck egg) is a snack food peddled everywhere; the *ulupong* is a poisonous snake often found in the *palayan* (rice field); *makisig* means handsome [man].

In Tagalog, the vowels are pronounced as in the Romance languages: *ah, ay, ee, owe, oo.* Hence pahn-**dahng**-go sah **ee**-lahw; **too**-too-bee; *mah*-kah-**hee**-yah; *sahm*-pah-**gee**-tah; mah-**gahn**-dahng bah-**bah**-ee; **rahm**-pah; bah-**loot**; **oo**-loo-pong; pah-**lah**-yahn; mah-**kee**-sig.

```
        the
      hands of
     the dancer
     the rays of
      the flame
       realize
        beauty
   as        pure        as
    the   tutubi rising   over
    the water and catching the
   moon on its cellophane wings
   stainless as rain on the palm
   trees of evening modest as shy                    these
   makahiya fine as a tourmaline      sky            hands that
      how she enchants us see          how           harvest hemp
   she   glances aside   as she weaves of            and cane that
   two  shining stars    a cincture       dig        the ditches
   of   firelight and                     and        check the
fay   a  magical purlieu               rampa            flow
see how    the goldenwhite              that        inch the garish
ribbons    of light hang in             hip        and silver jeepneys
          the air a garland            safe        through raucous chaos
          of sweet sampagita           feet        that mediate precarious
          to accent her grace          purchases on tumbling buses to
          magandang babae your         *balut!   balut! balut!* or risk
           dancing is like              the       fatal kiss of ulupong
            the play of                      mid   dark palayan   water
            the angel                        jog   under taxing    loads
            of light                      more meet for shandrydans
            bless us                      here find the perfect
           with  what                     form in dance to
          you    know                     celebrate a land
          the    soul                     prodigal of beauty
          of     art                      rich in grace salute
             and                          makisig this Elysian
             the                          wonder   honey-suckle
             joy                          lovely  at your side
              of                          raise   your lamp to
              it                          one   deserving of
                                          a   tribute far
                                          beyond our
                                          readiness to
                                          praise  dance
                                          like a     bird
                                          in air        you
                                            bear         the
                                             love        of
                                              all     of
                                               us
                                               for
                                               her
```

1492

The poem takes most of its details from what is allegedly Columbus's own account of his first voyage to America (see *The Log of Christopher Columbus,* trans. Robert H. Fuson, International Marine, 1987). Fearing Pinzon, captain of the *Pinta,* and a possible mutiny, Columbus was driven to ingenious lengths to persuade his men that landfall was near.

```
                        a
           ragtag   of
        fear  ridden         men     a
     delicate trio of        sea coffins
           here   on     a far reaching          sea      a
                go              and  no            backturning
     westward and trust to God        oh      may this daring
       adventure win through and      my              name  be
        inscribed in  the heavens with those of         my
        sovereign King  and his Queen by the will        of
         God monarchs of  Catholic Spain  we have for long days now
          had no sight of  land and the men  grow disgruntled still we
          press onward for  gold and innocent  souls to awaken to Christ
          in Whose hands is  our fate the wind  is strong and the compass
          always tells truth  the men are afraid  of a wind that will never
         blow east that will  hold them from home  in spite of their plaints
      I hold fast for the  Indies and tell them  the petrels and ringtails
      we see sleep ashore  stargrass and falling  stars promise that we are
      by land it heartens  them not and I cannot  trust Pinzon who yearning
     for glory is racing  forever ahead but the  sea makes up without wind
    an omen from God and  the men dare not rise  up against me the passing
                of       frigate birds assures  me that land must be near
                may   they guide us and soon  to the harbor we seek the
                crew                is       most anxious for landfall
                             and     reach it I shall with the
                           help                of
                                              our
                                              Lord
```

Spring

for Gary Frahm

This takes as its figure the Chinese ideogram for spring. *M[orchella] esculenta* is the morel mushroom. Ironically, Gary also first spotted the morel lurking within the figure.

```
                    when
                    lilac
                    verges    on the
                    edge of bloom and
                the leaf of the
            red oak's in the
        mouse ear stage
    first in the river      flat
  then where   the primal forest
    vaults   the vernal hill
            the beauties
            fruit fine
          M esculenta          gift
      of the April    gods quick
  in the ways of nature a good
    wise   soul instructs
          me in the mystery
          never let   them see
        your sack        until you
      can hold no         more silly
    maybe still I      do not doubt and
  keep it   out of     sight a long long while
  for I    am not   adept   at hunting them and add
          but a paltry     few to his rich harvest learn
          the art of        seeing he   advises when you look
        too hard         you cannot            see regard
      the finch        in flight the
    bloodroot's white and the vain
  sweet William's blue    and gold
morels     will leap         into the
eye life        he says         just let
          it come        to you and
          serving   up the bounty
          teaches me the proper
          grace to      praise
          the            feast
```

Carousel

for Evelyn Conley

```
            why is
     a    carousel sad
   and exact why is it
 turning forever around        in
my head? why is its music      its
movement as real as glass?     when
 if  at all will the melody    end?
  dreamlike my memories die    into
  animals   prancing around  in a
   formal   procession to nowhere
  calico   horses pace    up and                    down
   and a   tiger a     lion a zebra          move round
     to       the      music alongside a    bracket of swans as
            a    host of golden haired cherubs lean down from  the
             clouds and throw kisses  at cherubs that reaching from
             mirrors throw kisses at  them and the kisses are   lost
    on the    wind and the music and  movement and kisses all   waft
  over water to                   me                     in   this
   dream of a carousel wishes hitch  rides on the horses the lion
    the zebra parading past mirrors  where cherubs reach up from
    the sky     to throw kisses at cherubs who ride on the  soft
     light         of clouds and      kisses and horses     and
      wishes            ride          sadly around          and
        around         till             they waste         on
         the           wind              and music
          comes        over             the water
             to        call            in a   sigh
                       for             a circle
                        of             animals
                                    lost  in a
                                    song     on
                                    the
                                    wind
```

13

Madonna and Child

Christmas 2003

The Half-Moon Madonna and Child is a traditional design throughout the Christian world. My model, and the specific subject of the poem, was one carved by the Igorot people of the Philippines.

```
                serene in
             carved mahogany an
           Igorot Madonna swathes in
          pensive smiles her Holy Infant
         twenty centuries and untold worlds
         from Bethlehem how easily we    share
        her adoration love this gift  of  grace
       born of perfect modesty and   faith   to
       bring redemptive joy to a    hurt world
      yet we know that love        is never easy
    nor will all her love  spare Him the deep
    anguish of the Cross  another year draws
    to a clouded close  and still  we are
    no more moved to   loving truly  one
    another as we    do this Babe still
    we fail to   see  God's image drawn
    to life   in all    of those with
    whom     we share    the world
         may the day      come
    when we shall see          the end
    of this senseless       ceaseless war
    against ourselves      again the season
     comes to sing the    glory of the Prince
      of Peace again we     celebrate the hope
       and promise which    He brings to all
        may we find it in   ourselves to   be  as
         He has willed   may we know    a   love
          as pure as   hers and may   the Child
            cradled    gently   in   her heart
              as in her      arms    remind us
               that each time we  mark the
                 Holy Birth such   hope
                   is born anew
```

Sabbat

```
                    by
                    the
                    dark
                    power
                   of the
                   October
                   moon by
                   the holy
                   necessity
              of the season the
                sky is drained of
                  the  blood of the
                  setting sun the
                blood of our innocent sisters
                  comes alive in the healing light
                  of Hecate our sacred mother dancing
                      we draw down the moon and know the
power                 our venerable mothers knew who could
     concoct       a simple compound to induce the
         flow or break the fever's grip  bring
            the heavy crops to   harvest or
                  the grudging   babe to birth
                  so they   laugh and have it
                    that we fly on broomsticks
                    let them in the laughter
                    we are safe when however
                    they contend we hobnob with
                    the devil then it is we   need     fear
                    the rope the stones the    drowning pool how many
                    many times have we been     cursed and burned for
                    what we kenned by those    who took it ill that
                        women should be wise so   Hecate protect us
                        give us strength and teach us who we are
                        that we may share the ancient wisdom
                        mother     keep us     from all
                                            harm
```

In Memory: John Bennett

Poet, Melville scholar, satirist, John Bennett offered me my first teaching job; he died on Thanksgiving Day 1991. Among several other volumes, he wrote four books of poems on *Moby Dick* and *The Iambic Butterfly Net;* the latter and the idea of the butterfly as a traditional symbol of the soul and of resurrection suggested the poem's figure. The epigraph comes from the opening poem of his *Echoes from the Peaceable Kingdom:* "Old Adam, father, poet, priest" (Copyright © 1978 by Wm. B. Eerdmans Pub. Co., used by permission).

So now, Old Father, . . .
stand softly at the center of my skull
and chant your early metaphors of love
and set their joy against the bent world's rage.

```
      I
      write
     for love
     and loss a
     song for one
    who caught the
    delicate eternal
    beauty of an eden
  in a weave of iambs                          teacher
    wise enough to give            me leave to see
    my way you would not          let me know how near
      relentless death had        come but how could any
       net of merest flesh of worldstuff hope to hold
      your too-hard-loving too-long-drinking proverb
 of an Irish soul? it had to prove how it is death
 to be a poet death to love a poet and most surely
 death to insult a poet flinging knives of bitter
   rage at trousered apes who mocked the public
    trust or that first great command in Eden
     Watergate as well as whales could move
     your soul though sometimes to a caustic
     wit unworthy  of  the love that prompted
     it o voyager    with Ahab Flask Ishmael
       is your    farthest journey done?
       sweet    minstrel celebrant
        of        peace may you
                  know your
                   vision
                    now
```

Veteran's Day

Cupid's mother is, of course, Aphrodite (Venus).

```
        silly boy  a
     heart in one hand
     a dart in the other
    don't waste your easy        charm    on me
   wink your pretty cheeks       at giggly girls
   toss your frivolous darts     at awkward boys
  learning to play with theirs    squander your
   sweet nothings on the air     my pet oh what
     a kid I love ya baby be     my valentine
   go! I have no more heart       for  games
     the one I had's been         raked   a
         dozen times by        feral
            tigresses pierced
        by the cold spear of       a
       warrior queen gnawed        dry
      by harpies scarred and      worse
      until it learned to die      a
    hundred times and then to     laugh
  at   you       you and that bewitching
            queen your mother as  I
           laughed a rapier      wit
          born of a lively      woman
          touched my heart      as if
           aghast at drawing
            blood she used the
            surgeon's  vivifying
          art a dart    more keen
          than yours      to sew it
         new now my         puckish
        child you            see me
      so in love               your
      little                   prick
       is                      much
        too                       dull
```

21

Epithalamion

for Perry and Ivy

This wedding poem, written for two of my students, takes its shape from a traditional Pueblo Indian wedding vase. E.E. Cummings wrote: "since feeling is first/ who pays any attention/ to the syntax of things/ will never wholly kiss you."

```
you                                    who
have              taught            each
other         love   have          found
the joy    which         poets    priests
and madmen set            out resolutely
 to define yet           fall so short
 of realizing            ah you think
  no words can           ever capture
  what we feel           well feeling
   is first but       syntax isn't
    to be scorned   whatever late
    romantics theorize no kiss
    is really whole without it

    skill as well as love must
    shape the vessel just as a
    master touch    warrants the
   perfect vase  so  the exacting
   eye will see  most  clearly read
   the familiar  phrase  with keenest
   insight may   you read   deep in the
   texts each   other is the   secret all
   true love   confirms those   texts are
   richest   which will teach   us more
   the more we study them with love

    then shall this beginning mark
    what ever shall be new and
     ever more a wonder
```

The One That Got Away

or
more
likely
 that was
  never more   than   a
  ghostly visit   like a   coy
  dream that comes just on the   verge
  of waking not quite tangible enough to
  land a quivering shadow just beneath a
 quiet surface a flick of tail a quick eye
 a pouting   mouth toying with the snell
and then   only the slightest inkling
of a   disturbance in the water
                and   the feeling of a
                     promise somehow
                    made and broken
                  there had been of
                course no promise a
                hint a tease perhaps
              the way the Muse seduces
              offering a fleeting glimpse
            of ankle or of breast within a
            flowing veil and vanishing before
          we hear her whispers clearly and we
          are left to   dream the living flesh
          betrayed by the   phantom Muse   to
        follow   that which haunts us
        or find   what peace we can
      once having failed at   that
     uncommon and exacting art
     of   holding fast if
         intimation prove
           quicksilver

Wheatstraw

The design is taken from an actual piece of Bangladeshi wheatstraw art. The epigraph obviously owes much to Alexander Pope ("True wit is Nature to advantage dressed . . ."), as the closing lines do to "Rumpelstiltskin."

true
wit is nature
to advantage put
turning to profit
what is under
foot

it   is
past   poor
in Bangladesh the
women wealthy but
in   sun   in
pain   and   in a
myriad children far
too often hellish
floods   cradle
them in a
grisly   clutch
of branches recede to
leave but wrack and mud
and hunger in their track
from despair the women make
of that small portion dealt
them wheatstraw pictures of
a pretty world in which the
copper branches cradle owls   with
eyes as wide and quiet as   the
golden moon with feathers   rust
and russet yellow black   and bronze
a craft   to feed the hungry wide   and
quiet   eyes of children poor   are
the weapons of the poor and straw and
patience offer small defense from want
what mettle then with   such   frail
spears to stave off   such a
threat yet spinning   straw to
merchant gold the
anxious mothers
manage   dearth
from   less

27

A Song for St. Pat's

```
                    if all
                  the world
                be green me lads
              if all the world be
              green we'll have us
              the brawliest bash me
  lads   this      land has ever seen let
all the beer be     green lads and nary
a drop be spilt     let all the beer
 be green lads      and each one's cup  a
tilt if me lads     the beer be gone what?
 the beer be        gone? if the beer be
    gone            lads with the
  coming in           of dawn well  I
  will get us          more me lads
 I will get us     more because
 to drink green beer me lads
 is what the world is for
              drink aye and gustily      me
                lads and no man call a   stay
              drink up and heartily me   lads
              and the devil will happily  pay
             thus sang they all    and swilled
            they all and a tipsy    time was had
             and the tipplers all   laughed as
              the devil danced in   the head
             of every lad and what      he
             danced was giddy as       sin
             and their   feet were     set
            awry bite    me tongue     for
            saying it     but I can    not
            say a lie     they woke    up
              stupefied   in July     yes
              sometime    in July     and
            what they    woke         to
              required   a lot        of
              a sorely   addled       ken
             for it      seemed       as
            if a year    had gone     by
            and beer     was green
                           again
```

Lament for the Maker

Adolphe Sax, inventor of the saxophone, survived a fall from a third floor window as a child, lifelong poverty and ill health, an arsonist's torching of his workshop, and an assassin's attempt on his life. John Coltrane, Lester Young, and Charlie "Bird" Parker were great sax players.

```
                    sob in
                 the long cool
              winding  the soul
    your maker gave his    hurt was
 bled into you though      he never
                           heard the
                           long and
                           lonely of
                           a flight
                           by Coltrane
                           never felt
                           how Lester
                           eased the
                           strains of
                           purest pain
                           never knew
                           how "Bird"
                           taught his
                           heavy heart
                           to modulate         a
                           solo dance          of
                           gravesong           grieve
                           the boy in          deathlong
                           fall mourn          the hiss of
                           flames the          jealous whine
                           of bullets          sigh of what  a
                           man endured         of solitude
                           and hunger          to create a
                           voice the           very angels
                           must attend         and hearing
                           weep for us         improvise a
                           phrase into         a monody to
                           dignify that   ragged soul
                           who taught his agony to
                           sing and learned what
                           love can wring from
                              fall from flame
                               from fear
```

Toltec

The Figure in the Rug

The figure is of generic Toltec design, modeled loosely on the Warrior statues at the Temple of the Morning Star in Tula. Though the arms in those statures hang straight down and there are breastplates on their chests, the figure woven in the rug clearly has hands spread across his body.

```
         he must have been a consequential presence
         once                                    they
         made   him guard of the great pyramid   they
had raised to   honor a power they held in awe  but could not
         understand a god whose eye saw
all things who spoke in strange ways and who held the forces
of the vast sky  and sea in        hands they  could not reach
they sacrificed  to him what     they prayed  would be enough
to placate what  ill     will   they      may  have occasioned
quite by chance  by       one   act       of   trivial neglect
and they raised  the     tall   corn      and  plump beans and
caught the fish  that filled    the bellies  of their people
working not for  gold but for daughters and  sons to be safe
and playful but    most of        all not    to give offense
to him whose rage    changes     all the    world to stumbles
makes the mountains    roar and belch    out flame who keeps
             the   rains away  and
             turns  living  crops
             to powder    now woven
          in coarse wool his image
          is    commodified sold    to
          tourists as a curiosity from
             an        arcane age        as
          if     his only value was      to
          be          pleasing           to
          an     idle eye when hung      up
          in        a recess         or
             to   lie unseen waiting   as
             if      to trip us       as
             we cross the room what a
    falling off is here from guarding that most sacred temple
         to decorative art from pyramid to throw rug
         yet I praise him and give this modest recognition
                     to one
          who long ago provided some degree
             of security and comfort and
          the strength and courage to endure
```

33

Hélène de Nervo de Montgeroult

for Jim and Kathy March

A brilliant harpsichordist and composer, Hélène de Nervo, having been briefly married to the Marquis de Montgeroult, was imprisoned and condemned to the guillotine by the French Revolutionary Tribunal in 1793. Bernard Sarette, founder of the Paris Conservatoire, wanted her as a keyboard teacher for his new school, and risked his own life by pleading on her behalf. The President of the tribunal demanded that she play for the court, and despite her nine-month imprisonment she played with such intensity that the court spared her life. She fled to Berlin, but did later return to France and teach at the Conservatoire.

```
                       under the long shadow thrown by
                       that crude contraption made to
                       drink                   sweet
                       blood and toss off the spent
                       heads        to a jeering crowd
                       under          the cold sharp
                       glint            of a harsh
                       judge                   honed
                       to an                   angry
     biting edge   on      a dry               stone
     slicked now  with      blue               blood
     she was bid  to play                      after
     nine months   in hell without            light
     without any  music save the gnashing        of
     rats and of  bellies and moans of the damned
       her fingers  stiff galled starved for the touch of a
      keyboard to   play for her very life an instrument was
   brought before  that court of vengeance strange beauty in a
   den of jackals  and one bold champion she seized her chance
   quickly flexed   her long silent fingers sounded do re mi fa
   sol   la    ti do                                    and
   as    if    the     farce                  would     go
   no    as    if      dying                  nobly     in
    an   act   of      grace accorded welcome envoi     or
    as   if    to      touch ebony into sweet sound     to
   be          so      taken by joy    itself again     be
   of          all     fates most           fair there    as
    on          a      grand                stage     la
                       belle dame        like a wan
                       angel played   to the crude
                       court the Marseillaise and a
                       shout arose to let her live!
                       live!                  live!
```

Salamander

This poem, a chant based on the four classical elements and incorporating mythical and traditional as well as natural creatures, was suggested by a piece of Zuni silver. A *butiki* is a small gray lizard that often invades Filipino houses at night, walking especially on ceilings.

```
                    fire
               water air
                and earth
               born of fire
                      walks on
      water          light as
   air and heir      to earth
brother to the brontosaur
the thunder lizard born
    of stone brother to the
        bat-winged dragon power      of air
            and breath of fire sister to the
               swampland croc and desert dwelling
    Gila      monster sister to the whip tailed racer
slick as cornsilk   quick as wind kin        to silver
  butiki ceiling        tracker come by        night
    blood of            horrid basilisk      born of
  cockerel              hatched by snake       eye
    whose               very glance is death
                        distant   kindred too of
                        phoenix     rising new from
                         flaming        ash promise of
                          eternal           being  artifice
                           of Zuni           silver born anew
                           of earth                and fire air
                           water                            earth
                                                               and
                                                             fire
```

A Posy

for Annette, fighting cancer

bloom   you
jauntiness   of color
throw your acid blue and
pink   amethyst and raucous red
open for the sun the butterfly the
wind the bee who seeks to churn your
essence to the   sweetest gold
bloom not for   that lovesick
girl whose   sighs threaten
to unhinge   the world she
will only tear   your petals one
by one to learn what she already
knows that for the loving
young the world is love
and   even pain
can   be the
warmest   joy
no bloom instead   for   those
who live with pain that   knows no
joy knows only the grim anguish   of a sickness
that   eats away within   relentlessly
splash your brazen rainbow
across   that shadow
scream   the
gospel
verity
of hope
and let
them know that even from a seed
deep in the darkness can burst forth
a blaze of color to defy
the dark

The Lesson of the Snow

Christmas 2006

```
          softly
         the snow's
          eternal white    descends
           to wrap the soiled earth
             in sparkling innocence
             what are we to make of
             all this gifting this
               new beginning? will  we
               wonder only for a moment
             then shout curses as cars
           skid out of our control or
           fingers  freeze?  watch
                the    children    lie
               down and figure angels
             in the snow and rising
                  erase   all   traces
             of the fall    did not
           He who came to free us
      say    we must become as they? what
   can    it mean but to embrace the glory
 in the gift? and there it   is the wonder
    such a    freshness full   of angels now
             their breathing visible they make
         of snow a simple likeness of a man
         attentive to this new creation they
         bestow a rag scarf   and dashing hat
         and a red beet nose   and laughing do
         not mind that all his days are surely
         numbered with what felicity they can
         receive each moment's richness even
         as their snowman   touched by some
           transforming and   glorious light
           begins to melt away is this not
           too a lesson from the snow? it
             lives as man for one brief
             day and then returns to
                its essential state
```

Winner

for Tash

```
                    it
                  was a
                lively one
              the year that
            she   got Cinnamon
          for Christmas oh she
         rode him long and hard
       and fast   and when I asked              her
     why she      rode so furiously       she couldn't say
   where            she was going she would only laugh and say
       away         she was three then now she's twenty-three and
            drives a red Fiero (Cyclops for the light that  will not
                  close) but not thank God so hard so   fast yet
                  still away although today she knows      where
                  she is going sits the saddle firmly        rides
                  with confidence and grace prepared
                  to face   whatever comes     for us
                what                             comes
                into                              this
                room                             (now
   she is         gone                            from       it) is
     silence mostly                              for her it was
         time to go and                        she'll do fine
            Cinnamon rests              easy now rocks
                only if a hand should chance to
                          brush him
```

Sunday Bridge

```
                a
               bid
              slips
             timidly
            into what          a
           cute sarong        one
          club I found in    Kay's
         the other day sorry  did you
        bid? a club I wonder  if I pass
         Jeanette has seen  a spade her
           brother double  Alan's doctor
            said I pass  he shouldn't go
             to Denver  with two diamonds
              Richard  pass is Ina getting
               ready  for four hearts I saw
                her   fiancé the I don't have
                 a    lead oh you always have
                  the kings  I  never get
    I see      Maria   bought   a   why is
 Princess     barking?          she
just wants   to did you        catch
the morning news on six
this Shelley's class is  how
you bid weak twos that  lemon
 cake was scrumptious  did you
  open? will you let  me have I
  can't remember if  two clubs
   you name the      longer of
    two spades did  Mildred   get
     her four  spades Harry  thinks
     I need  new that  was my trick
      Eva's  hollyhocks are gorgeous
      have  you seen them? down two
      are   we playing Wednesday?
      I     can't make it Amy's
            booked  a  coffee
             for   a   man
                  who
                 wants
```

Terpsichore's Darling

Terpsichore, the Muse of dance, is one of the nine "daughters of Memory" (Mnemosyne). The Irish poet is W.B. Yeats; the quotation is taken from his poem, "Adam's Curse."

<pre>
as
 her
  toes
   point
    saucily
     toward
      a star
       unseen
        except
         in her
          dreams   what
           thoughts   are dancing
          in her cyan   eyes? does she
         see   that all   those hours that
          time and pain   shape the way to
          grace and ease   and beauty? that
          fitful tears in   failure buoy the
          lift of art? one   who thinks to
         win the   favor of   the Muse   and
         not to   work has   little
        regard   for what   excites her
       she is   difficult to   woo and proudly
      expects   her favor will   be earned if there
     are some   who share a closeness to the daughters
   of Memory still *there is no fine thing since Adam's fall* as the
   Irish poet understood *but needs much laboring* solely by absolute
   surrender to the Muse could   she attain such talent a fine form
   without betraying the slightest strain adorned with a smile and
                         winsomeness so radiant we rejoice but
                           seldom   think what the cost has
                                     been
</pre>

Eye of God

for Robert J. Conley

The story told here is an adaptation of a Bolivian Indian legend of the origin of the *Ojo de Dios*.

to her
it was
as
though
dark stole
the world away
her mother prayed:
what can I do that my
dear child   might know
again eyes   quick with
the things   of   day? after
three long   nights   her answer
came: you must bring down the rainbow from
the sky or blindness will be with her always
afraid she   dared not think it was   impossible
she had to   find a way to draw the   color down
but how? three   fretful days she agonized   before she saw
then gleaning   a bouquet of   azure violet   bright indigo
yew and yellow   emerald ruby marigold and   vermillion wed
the colors   with a yarn she'd spun   of llama's
wool fixed   a frame of two crossed   sticks and
thus began to weave her vision as   she worked
a rainbow left the sky and filled that eye
with light   humble   before the
miracle of   it   she waited
for a sign   would this
bring back   the day to
stoneblind eyes? from
her side came soft
words sweet as
music: the
sky is
so
pretty
mother

Icon

This poem is written in an approximation of the Middle English alliterative line:

> Lancelot, verily longing   to serve well his Lord,
> Righteous did ride   for the realm of Arthur. . . .

The allusion is to *Sir Gawain and the Green Knight*, ll. 648-50 (Borroff trans.):

> And therefore, as I find, he fittingly had
> On the inner part of his shield her image portrayed,
> That when his look on it lighted, he never lost heart.

```
                    Lancelot
               verily longing
              to serve well his
              Lord righteous did
              ride for the realm
              of Arthur bearing
              ever before him the
              pure blessed image
             of heaven's queen
             heart proud and
            blazons held
          high so too Gawain
        gazed    on the glorious
              Virgin pressing his
              weary way through the
              Cheshire wild fated
              soon to feel that              fatal
           bite    of the axe          now chrome
          on a      carrier's       mudflap claims
          that      devotion      a fabulous figure
         full       and fair     to knights    of the
         road       if Gawain   didn't give    in and
        came        into grace  Lance less      chaste
        knew        lust with his liege's           queen
        are         we so different after all? do we      then
       aim          less high? should we for boorishness    feel
      shame         or shun shapeliness? no the  burden has    been
    ever    so         though for our buxom          beauty no Camelot
                       will cleave                    nor kingdom
                                                      blaze
```

51

Frazzled

This was written for a fourth grade class, which suggested a poem in the shape of a squirrel. A member of that class told me the joke quoted in the poem.

```
                                      ah
                                    me those
                                  awful jokes
            that I                get told  all
         the time "Why            did the chicken
       cross the road?"           "To prove to the
     squirrel it could be          done" what can
   I do? I keep after the         kids all the
  time tell them they have       to be careful    but
 do they listen? no and the     traffic's just  awful
people will brake for dogs    for cats! but never
for us what do we ever do    to them? okay so we
chew on a    cable every   now and again raise
hob with      the phone   service so that's a
 reason        to run us   down? I keep telling
  them       stay away    from the street keep
           out of the   traffic they can run
         all day in   the trees cavorting
        and racing   from limb to limb    and
       never fall   never but they don't want
       to do that   or they can tightrope the
       power line   if they just have to get
       across the   road but oh no not them
       they go on   playing chicken in the
       street with   speeding cars what's
       a nerveworn   mother to do? now
        I hear tell   they're going to widen
          the bloody   road I bet even the
            chicken    won't be able
                          to make it
                            then
```

Designs—9/11

This poem was twice an accident of history. I had drafted the design for a poem on the evolution of human self-expression, and written about two-thirds of it, but didn't know how to end it, and so set it aside. The attack on the Twin Towers gave a focus for an ending, and the poem was finished when American resolve was strengthened by an outpouring of international support. Then came the ill-advised invasion of Iraq, and I fear the poem may now read as an exercise in nationalistic jingoism. It certainly was not intended to be.

```
            first
        blood drawn
            on rock ash
              on clay say                              I
                am I will                            mark
                  the world                      make it
                  aware of                     me express
                  my fears                    try to please
                    whatever            gods may   watch      a
                      spelling    alphabet         opens      up
                      new ways  to name            makes      it
                          possible                             for
stories laws and science to be  set free  of time and voice spring from
mind to mind until the universe  explodes  with possibilities and from a
quill a new nation rises born of  words We  the people hold these truths
                            and with                          axe
                and plow      arm and              dream      we
                create a          nation            which     if
              yet imperfect flashes  tall in glass and steel   a
              vision of generous wealth  at  heart shaped by an
          idea so resplendent it allows  a  people to withstand
                                a
                            martyrdom
                            etched
                            in flames
                            and hatred
```

Laureate

```
6:15 a.m. at the local pancake spot
 he sips bad coffee tries to think
  of what to say to folks who see
  the sun rise every morning nods
  a sort of thanks to the perky waitress
  who has filled his cup before he can say
  no stares at the egg congealing      in a
  greasy pool  before   his heavy      eyes
  listens to    the     easy banter    talk
  of bowling        fish that got      away
  some comic    on   Jay Leno and      asks
  himself if   this   is worth it      what
  droll muse   would   ever exact      such
  tribute? a   shiver   calls him      back
  he is here   to read   to these      guys
  they'd even  made him  laureate      only
  club to have one still he feels     like
  he's intruding even though they     have
  invited him how can he find a common
  language? the gavel falls all rise
  recite the pledge he waits while
  routine business is attended to
   then introduced he stands and
      understands as one by one
          they rise apologize
            and leave for
                  work
                  till
                 facing
            the stalwart few
   he clears his throat I wrote
  this one when I found the word
```

57

Seconds

                    like
                  so much
                  else in
                    life   it all
                                                               hangs on a
                                                  split   second on the
                                                  speed   of the ball   a
                                                  twist   of a wrist   or
                                                 phrase   which   will
           fix   forever   the outcome of   the
        game and one is suddenly out   out of time of   luck
       of love the slightest slip of   the foot or the tongue
         and   it is too late there   is no going back no erasing
                            the words nor putting the blood back in the
                 drained   heart only by grace or error can we
            be safe a dropped ball a missed tag a forgiveness
   is the best   we dare hope for in this bruised world
   the thinnest   chance that lets us somehow
                        slide home free

Noël

The design for this poem, written as a Christmas card in 2001, was taken from an antique weathervane in Pennsylvania. It is written in tetrameter quatrains.

```
         again
           this year
             the angels
               sing again
                 proclaim Noël
                   on earth again
   we greet our        holy King again
     are humbled by His birth still the
       dark that held the star still our
           aching hearts in waiting still
             the frankincense and myrrh     still
               a glory radiating this   time will                a
                 spirit stir us?   this time is        the       inn
                   prepared? this time will His truth inspire us? this
                   time will His life be spared?     when        the
                 night betrays the day when He      dies         a
               broken man when the stone is rolled    away
       is                    when at last we know His   plan
     but now we celebrate His birth now acknowledge once again
   God has come to live as man God to walk with us  on earth
 in        this season's splendid promise may       all
     we  fear be kept far from us still Your
   precious Son professing may our faith
 and joy increase again made mindful
of    Your blessing still O Lord
     we pray for peace Amen
```

Carousel II: Legends

for Brooklyn

The carousel across the lake from where I grew up (see "Carousel," p. 12) was later moved to Cedar Point in Ohio. During its years there, several people reported seeing a ghost coming at night to ride its "Military" horse, a black steed, and several legends grew up around it. When the carousel was later sold and moved to Pennsylvania, that "ghost" horse was kept on display in Cedar Point and a replica put in its place.

                    in
                 the night
                 the carousel is
                 still except when she
                 arrives and makes her
                 liquid way unerringly
                 through the silent dark
            to   the black as she mounts
            him   a pale light like sea
            fog   visible comes   up
            the   carousel begins
            its   necessary rounds
            who   is she? why does
      she come   to that horse? some who've
   seen her say she rode it with her love before he left
   for war they were to wed when he came back but he did not
   come back now she comes to live again that blessed promise   which
   is all she has of him this constant lonely ghostly ride to somewhere
   else some say the charger was the favorite of its maker's wife   that
   she   might be   the   phantom   lady
   who   comes to ride alone by night to touch again the joy   she
   knew   the gift of love her husband carved into the horse   should
    you   see this as so much wistful nonsense consider this   when
    the   carousel was   sold   a replica
    was   settled in   his   place and
    he   stayed here   now   he rests
        immobile pent   and   cannot
        canter   with   his   misty
        wraith   does   she   ever
         still   long   to   ride
          him?   since   that
          day   she   has
          not   been
         seen

Having grown up in a letterpress print shop in small town
Michigan, Jan D. Hodge received his BA and MA degrees
from the University of Michigan and his PhD from
the University of New Mexico,
where he wrote his dissertation on Charles Dickens.
He taught at Rockford (Illinois) College
and at Morningside College in Sioux City, Iowa.
His poems have appeared in *Iambs & Trochees,*
American Arts Quarterly, Defined Providence,
and many other print and online journals.

ALSO FROM ABLE MUSE PRESS

William Baer, *Times Square and Other Stories*

Melissa Balmain, *Walking in on People – Poems*

Ben Berman, *Strange Borderlands – Poems*

Michael Cantor, *Life in the Second Circle – Poems*

Catherine Chandler, *Lines of Flight – Poems*

William Conelly, *Uncontested Grounds – Poems*

Maryann Corbett,
    Credo for the Checkout Line in Winter – Poems

John Philip Drury, *Sea Level Rising – Poems*

D.R. Goodman, *Greed: A Confession – Poems*

Margaret Ann Griffiths,
    Grasshopper – The Poetry of M A Griffiths

Ellen Kaufman, *House Music – Poems*

Carol Light, *Heaven from Steam – Poems*

April Lindner, *This Bed Our Bodies Shaped – Poems*

Martin McGovern, *Bad Fame – Poems*

Jeredith Merrin, *Cup – Poems*

Richard Newman,
    All the Wasted Beauty of the World – Poems

Frank Osen, *Virtue, Big as Sin – Poems*

Alexander Pepple (Editor), *Able Muse Anthology*

Alexander Pepple (Editor),
    Able Muse – a review of poetry, prose & art
    (semiannual issues, Winter 2010 onward)

James Pollock, *Sailing to Babylon – Poems*

Aaron Poochigian, *The Cosmic Purr – Poems*

John Ridland,
    Sir Gawain and the Green Knight – Translation

Stephen Scaer, *Pumpkin Chucking – Poems*

Hollis Seamon, *Corporeality – Stories*

Carrie Shipers, *Embarking on Catastrophe – Poems*

Matthew Buckley Smith,
    Dirge for an Imaginary World – Poems

Barbara Ellen Sorensen,
    Compositions of the Dead Playing Flutes – Poems

Wendy Videlock, *Slingshots and Love Plums – Poems*

Wendy Videlock, *The Dark Gnu and Other Poems*

Wendy Videlock, *Nevertheless – Poems*

Richard Wakefield, *A Vertical Mile – Poems*

Gail White, *Asperity Street – Poems*

Chelsea Woodard, *Vellum – Poems*

www.ablemusepress.com

www.ingramcontent.com/pod-product-compliance
Lightning Source LLC
Chambersburg PA
CBHW080540090426
42733CB00016B/2636